easy
indian
in minutes

This edition printed in 2008 for
Bookmart Ltd
Blaby Road
Wigston
Leicester LE18 4SE

First published in Great Britain in 2005 by
Kyle Cathie Ltd for Sainsbury's Supermarkets Ltd

10 9 8 7 6 5 4 3 2 1

ISBN: 978 1 85626 893 6

Senior editor Helen Woodhall
Designer: Geoff Hayes
Styling: Penny Markham
Home Economist: Annie Nichols
Production: Sha Huxtable and Alice Holloway

With thanks and acknowlegement to all the recipe writers
whose talents have contributed to the creation of this book.

With special thanks to Linda Bain, Nicola Donovan, Amanda Fries,
Sarah Lee and Kate McBain.

Colour reproduction by Scanhouse Pty Ltd
Printed and bound in China by C & C Offset Printers

**The eggs used in this book are medium sized. All spoon
measurements for dry ingredients are heaped.**

contents

introduction – the best of indian food

The taste of Indian food as we know it in the UK is a surprisingly British thing. There's no direct translation of the word 'curry' – it may come from kari, a spicy tamarind sauce, or karai, a frying pan used to prepare spices, but it isn't known in India. Nor indeed are favourites such as chicken tikka masala and balti dishes, which are part of the phenomenon known as Brit-Indie cooking.

Indian food is familiar through restaurants and takeaways – Onion Bhajis (see page 18) and Chicken Korma (page 50) rank among the nation's favourite foods – but many are nervous about cooking Indian food at home. Perhaps it's because of the unfamiliar ingredients or the common misconception that Indian food should be hot enough to give you a hernia. But in fact, as you will see in the pages of this book, preparing delicious Indian dishes can be quick, easy and immensely satisfying. After all, many 'curries' are simply spicy stews of tender meat braised in an aromatic gravy. So stock up your spice rack and get to grips with Indian cuisine in your own home.

Spices

Spices are at the heart and soul of Indian cooking and knowing how to use them is the key to producing delicious Indian meals. Skilful blending creates alluring aromas and magical flavours, with the spices enhancing the main ingredients. No single spice should dominate the dishes we've chosen here.

Freshness is vital, too. It's best to buy small quantities of spices and store them in a cool dry place in an airtight container, replacing them every six months so that they keep the flavour. Buy whole seeds and pods of spices such as cumin and cardamom if you can. Fry them for a few seconds, allow them to cool, then crush them in a pestle and mortar – they'll have a richer, deeper flavour than ready-ground powders.

Whatever the dish you are preparing, always fry your spices before the vegetables or meat to release their flavours and eliminate any raw taste. Be careful not to cook spices for too long, otherwise their flavours will become unpleasantly bitter.

Vegetables and pulses

These are crucial ingredients in a country where up to 80 per cent of the population is vegetarian, and of course they are healthy and asty too. Many of the vegetables used in Indian cooking are old British favourites given a new twist, as in Sag Aloo with Cottage Cheese (page 3) or the crunchy Carrot and Cauliflower relish on page 16 or Spiced Pumpkin and Cauliflower on page 78. Don't be afraid to experiment, either – if you have never cooked sweet potato or okra, turn to Sweet Potato and Mango Jalfrezi (page 36) and Okra Stir-fry (page 82) for some new taste sensations.

Pulses such as lentils and chickpeas form the basis of many dishes in a vegetarian household. So important are they to the Indian diet that while westerners talk of earning their 'daily bread', Indians earn their dhal roti ('lentil bread'). Pulses are both cheap and nutritious, a great source of low-fat protein for those wanting to follow a healthy vegetarian diet, and, because variety is the spice of life, there are thousands of regional takes on basic dishes – try Lentil-stuffed Mushrooms (page 90), Chickpeas with Raita (page 92) or Dahl (page 95).

Staples

The most popular type of rice in India is Basmati, which may be boiled to soak up the luscious flavours of the main dishes, but is also the basis for pilau, made by soaking the rice in water, frying it lightly, then boiling it with different vegetables and spices. Pilau Rice with Cashews (page 102), Vegetable Pilau (page 104) and Green Pea Pilau (page 106) show just how versatile this simple ingredient can be.

But Indian food doesn't mean 'rice with everything'. Breads such as naan, paratha and chapati are popular in the drier parts of the country, where rice doesn't grow. These are quite difficult to make at home, so it's probably better to buy them ready-made, but we have included recipes for wholemeal Pooris (page 98) and Potato Breads (page 100) in case you want to have a go.

Meat and fish

Eating meat and fish has become more widespread in India as meat has become more readily available. Goat, lamb and chicken are the most popular. Few Indians possess a tandoor – a charcoal-fired clay oven – so for this style of cooking they use a barbecue or grill. The meat is marinated in spices, often mixed with yogurt to produce a coating texture, then cooked in a matter of minutes over a high heat. Tikka Chicken (page 54) and Marinated Lamb Chops (page 56) are two easy dishes prepared in this way, with the spicy marinade adding a special something to everyday ingredients.

For those living along the coast or the fishing rivers of India, many different types of fish are bought and cooked within hours of being landed. Like meat and poultry, fish and seafood may be 'curried' in a sauce or marinated before being grilled or fried. Alternatively, for a real taste of the Raj, try our variation on that great brunch dish, kedgeree (page 46).

Side dishes
No Indian meal is complete without pickles, chutneys and raitas to accompany the main dishes. Yogurt-based raitas (page 14) are the ideal companion to spicy food. Bhajis, samosas and pakoras are street food, sold at the roadside to be eaten in the fingers, but in this country we have adopted many favourites as starters or side dishes. Traditionally fried, they can be made in reduced-fat versions by baking in a hot oven. Try Mushroom Bhajis (page 20), Turkey Samosas (page 22) or our special Pakora Platter with Spicy Dip (page 26).

Types of curry
How hot can you take it? If the answer is not very, stick to kormas and masalas. Otherwise, the sky is your limit. Here's a quick rundown on the various types of curry you will find in this book, starting with the mildest and stoking up the heat as we go along.

Korma: a technique from northern India that means braising to produce alluring flavours in creamy sauce. The korma's secret lies in marinating meat in a spice-laced yogurt mixture before braising. Western versions are mild and creamy, with almonds. Try Chicken Korma (page 50) or Cauliflower Korma (page 81).

Masala: a mild, creamy curry, similar to the korma with the addition of tomatoes. A good starting point if you are nervous of spices and chilli. Try Mussels Masala (page 45).

Tikka: chunks of meat, fish or vegetables marinated in spices and yogurt, then skewered and cooked in a tandoor, under a grill or on a barbecue. Tikka dishes are often served in the West as a starter or as part of a mixed grill. Try Tikka Chicken (page 54).

Balti: a one-pot curry dish introduced to the UK by Kashmiris. A balti is essentially a stir-fry curry made quickly with fresh marinated ingredients, cooked and served in a balti or 'bucket'. Try Balti Chicken (page 52).

Madras: a hot, tomato-based curry from southern India. Try Aubergine Madras (page 34

alfrezi: a hot spicy dish that originated
in the Raj, made with green pepper, chilli,
onion and tomato, together with sautéed
chicken or vegetables. Not for the faint-
hearted. Try Sweet Potato and Mango
alfrezi (page 36).

sweet dishes

Sweets and puddings are considered 'foods of
the gods' and are eaten at teatime or at dinner
parties and banquets. An everyday meal might
end with fruit or ice cream, or with a delicious
yoghurt-based drink called a lassi (page 121)
flavoured with fruit and served either sweet or
salty – a perfect digestif after a rich meal.

HOW TO USE THIS BOOK: A typical Indian
meal is likely to consist of one or two
vegetable dishes, a meat dish, rice or bread
and relishes, all served at the same time, but
for those of you who prefer the Western
approach of a starter followed by a main dish,
the chapters are divided into the courses of
the meal, with separate sections on
vegetables and on rice and bread. We have
given preparation and cooking times to help
with planning and, as a guide, there are also
calorie and fat counts for each dish.

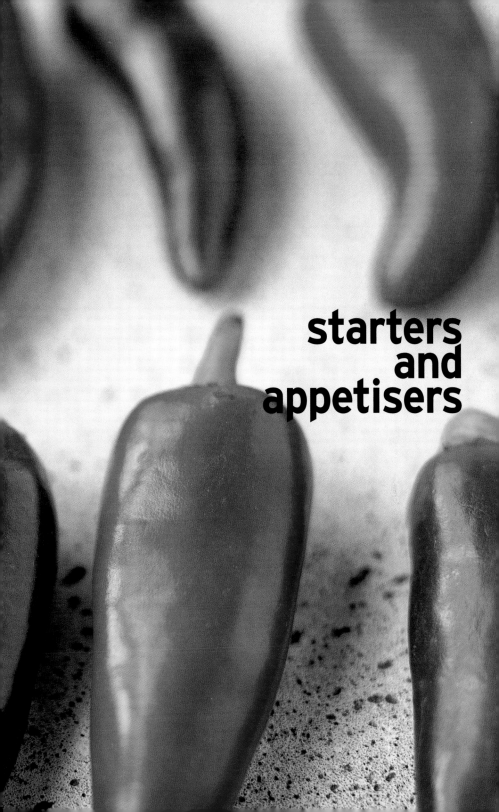

**starters
and
appetisers**

cucumber raita (*right*)

Cool and creamy raita is perfect with spicy poppadoms.

prep time | serves 3-4 | 25 cals per serving | 0.4g fat per serving

1/4 cucumber, deseeded and finely chopped
150g (5oz) low-fat natural yogurt
1/2 x 20g (3/4oz) pack mint, roughly chopped
pinch ground cumin

Place all the above ingredients in a bowl, reserving a little cucumber and mint. Mix to combine. Garnish with cucumber and mint and serve with poppadoms or as an accompaniment.

pistachio raita

A nutty raita with a hint of sweetness.

prep time | serves 4-6 | 91 cals per serving | 3g fat per serving

500g (1lb) low-fat natural yogurt
4 tablespoons rose-water
2 tablespoons clear honey
20g (3/4oz) unsalted shelled pistachio nuts, chopped
pinch ground saffron or a few saffron strands soaked for a few minutes

Put the yogurt in a bowl and stir in the rose-water, honey and pistachios. Chill in the refrigerator until required.

Just before serving, drain the saffron, sprinkle over the raita and serve.

spiced almonds

So more-ish! These super-tasty nuts go wonderfully with a pre-dinner drink.

prep & cook time	serves 6	per serving	per serving
15 mins		197 cals	19g fat

3 tablespoons sunflower oil
125g (4oz) flaked almonds
1 teaspoon salt
1 teaspoon curry powder

Heat the oil in a frying pan, add the almonds and fry gently for 2-3 minutes until golden brown. Drain on kitchen paper, then place in a serving dish.

Mix the salt and curry powder together and sprinkle over the almonds, tossing well to coat.

carrot and cauliflower relish

A crunchy chutney with a touch of spice.

prep & cook time	serves 4-6	per serving	per serving
1½ hrs		39 cals	2g fat

175g (6oz) cauliflower florets
3 carrots, peeled and sliced
1 teaspoon vegetable oil
½ teaspoon ground turmeric
1 teaspoon chilli powder
1 teaspoon sugar
4 tablespoons tarragon vinegar
1 teaspoon mustard seeds

Blanch the cauliflower and carrots in boiling water for 1 minute. Refresh in cold water.

Combine all the remaining ingredients in a large bowl. Add the vegetables and leave to stand for about 1 hour, allowing the cauliflower and carrots to absorb the various flavours.

Serve cooled, but not chilled, as this would impair the flavour.

onion bhajis

Everybody's favourite, whether you serve them as a starter or with other dishes as part of the main course.

20 mins prep & cook time　　**serves 6**　　**119 cals** per serving　　**6g fat** per serving

1 large egg
1 tablespoon lemon juice
8 tablespoons cold water
175g (6oz) plain flour
1 teaspoon ground cumin
$1/2$ teaspoon turmeric
$1^1/2$-2 teaspoons chilli powder
1 teaspoon garam masala
$1^1/2$ teaspoon salt
175g (6oz) onions, finely sliced
lemon wedges

Break the egg into a small bowl, add the lemon juice and water and whisk lightly together.

In another bowl, sieve the flour and spices together, then stir in the salt. Make a well in the centre of the flour and pour in the egg mixture. Using a fork, gradually incorporate the flour into the liquid until a thick batter is formed. Leave to stand for 10-15 minutes.

Heat the oil in a deep-fat fryer until it reaches 170°C/325°F.

Stir the onions into the batter, lower rounded tablespoons of the mixture carefully into the hot oil and cook for approximately 4 minutes, turning the bhajis frequently with a slotted metal spoon.

Remove from the oil and drain on kitchen pa Serve immediately with lemon wedges and of the dips on pages 14 or 24.

Variation
Use a batter mix in place of the flour, water lemon juice if you prefer.

mushroom bhaji

A quick and easy vegetable dish that's ready in minutes.

15 mins — prep & cook time

serves 2

284 cals — per serving

29g fat — per serving

4 tablespoons oil
250g (8oz) button mushrooms, wiped
2 teaspoons tomato purée
2 teaspoons garam masala
a few coriander leaves, shredded
2 naan breads

Heat the oil in a frying pan, and gently cook the mushrooms for about 4 minutes, or until soft.

Add the tomato purée, garam masala and coriander leaves. Stir-fry for 1-2 minutes, then serve with warm naan bread.

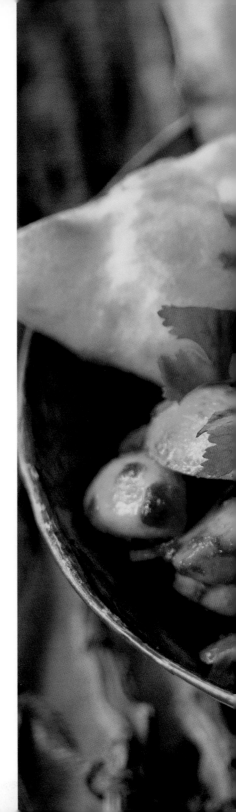

turkey samosas

Baking rather than deep-frying keeps samosas light and healthy.

45 mins — prep & cook time

makes 16

82 cals — per serving

5g fat — per serving

2 tablespoons sunflower oil
450g (15oz) turkey mince
2 tablespoons medium curry paste
1 tablespoon cumin seeds
1 tablespoon tomato purée
1 onion, finely chopped
lemon juice, to taste
8 sheets filo pastry
3 tablespoons melted butter
salt and freshly ground black pepper

Preheat the oven to 220°C/425°F/gas mark 7.

Heat the oil in a frying pan. Add the turkey mince and stir fry for 2-3 minutes. Add the curry paste and cumin seeds and stir fry for 1 minute.

Add the remaining ingredients (except the pastry and butter) and mix in.

Cut each strip of filo pastry in half, lengthways. Brush with melted butter. Place a spoonful of turkey mixture onto the top corner of each slice and fold over to form a triangle. Keep folding around to use all the pastry strip.

Place on a baking tray and bake for 10-15 minutes until crisp and golden. Serve immediately.

split pea balls with cucumber & mint dip

Delicious on their own or stuffed into a split naan for a quick snack.

45 mins	serves 4	**265** cals	**3**g fat
prep & cook time	serves 4	per serving	per serving

125g (4oz) yellow split peas, soaked overnight
125g (4oz) green split peas, soaked overnight
1 x 20g (³/₄oz) pack coriander, roughly chopped
1 bird's eye chilli, deseeded and finely chopped
1 teaspoon garam masala
1 egg
1 tablespoon semolina

For the dip:
150g (5oz) low-fat natural yogurt
1 small cucumber, deseeded and chopped
1 x 20g (³/₄oz) pack fresh mint, finely chopped
salt and freshly ground black pepper

Cook the split peas for 35-45 minutes until soft, then drain and cool. Place in a food processor along with the coriander, chilli, garam masala, seasoning and egg. Process until smooth.

Preheat the oven to 220°C/425°F/gas mark 7.

Divide the mixture into 16 pieces, shape into balls, then roll in semolina. Transfer to a foil-lined baking sheet and place in the oven. Cook for 15-20 minutes.

Combine the yogurt, cucumber and mint and place in a bowl. Serve with the split pea balls.

pakora platter with spicy dip

Great for entertaining a crowd - place in the middle of the table and let everyone help themselves.

30 mins		225 cals	11g fat
prep & cook time	serves 4-6	per serving	per serving

150g (5oz) plain flour
1 teaspoon turmeric
1 teaspoon whole cumin seeds, lightly toasted, then ground
1 teaspoon fennel seeds, lightly toasted, then ground
1 teaspoon garam masala
salt and freshly ground black pepper
1 x 20g (³/₄oz) pack fresh coriander, finely chopped
1 egg, beaten
150ml (5fl oz) milk
50g (2oz) butter, melted
100g (3¹/₂oz) okra, topped and tailed, then cut into rings
2 carrots, peeled and coarsely grated
1 courgette, coarsely grated

2 tablespoons aubergine chutney
150ml (5fl oz) natural yogurt

Preheat a deep-fat fryer to 190°C/375°F.

In a bowl combine together the first seven ingredients, then add the egg, milk and butter and mix to form a stiff batter.

Add the vegetables and mix to incorporate all the ingredients. Drop spoonfuls of the mixture into the deep-fat fryer and cook for 1-2 minute until golden brown. Drain on absorbent kitchen paper and keep warm whilst frying the remain batches.

To make the dipping sauce, combine the chutn and natural yogurt. Transfer to a serving bowl.

Serve the spicy vegetable pakoras on a platter alongside the dip.

rava dosa with cumin dhal and coriander

A dosa is a type of pancake from southern India. This delicious dis
combines the pancakes with a delicately spiced dhal.

45 mins	serves 4	431 cals	12g fat
prep & cook time	serves 4	per serving	per serving

For the cumin dhal:
500g (1lb) yellow split peas
2 tablespoons olive oil
4 cloves garlic, finely chopped
2.5cm (1in) piece ginger, grated
2 red chillies, deseeded and chopped
2 teaspoons ground cumin
2 teaspoons ground turmeric
2 litres (3½ pints) water
salt

For the rava dosa pancakes:
100g (3½oz) self-raising flour
100g (3½oz) semolina
100g (3½oz) polenta
2 teaspoons toasted cumin seeds
1 teaspoon turmeric
400ml (14fl oz) water
salt

2 tablespoons vegetable oil for frying
1 x 20g (¾oz) pack fresh coriander
100ml (3½fl oz) natural yogurt, optional

To make the dhal, rinse the yellow split peas and discard any small stones.

Heat the olive oil in a saucepan over a moderate heat and fry the garlic, ginger and chillies for 1-2 minutes.

Add the cumin and turmeric and continue to cook for 1 minute.

Add the yellow split peas and stir well, then a
the water and bring to the boil. Reduce the he
to a simmer, and cook, stirring occasionally, fo
30-40 minutes.

Season with salt, remove from the heat and s
aside.

To make the pancakes, mix all the dry ingredients together, pour in the water, and whisk to form a smooth batter.

Lightly oil a heavy-based frying pan, and place over a moderate heat. Pour small amou
of the mixture into the middle of the pan and tilt the pan to allow the mixture to spread to the edges.

When bubbles appear on the surface, flip the pancake over with a palette knife and cook for
further minute. Repeat this with the rest of th
pancake mixture.

To serve, slide a pancake onto a plate. Place 2
spoonfuls of dhal in the middle, put a tablespo
of yogurt on top (if using), and 1-2 sprigs of coriander. Fold over the top and the sides, and
roll into sausage shapes.

main
courses

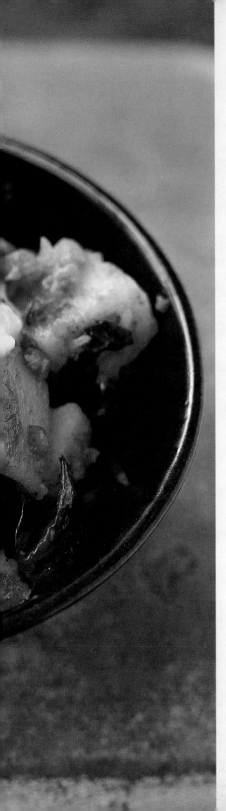

saag aloo with cottage cheese

A light and fresh vegetable dish packed with goodness and flavour.

30 mins prep & cook time   serves 2   **270 cals** per serving   **10g fat** per serving

1 tablespoon groundnut oil
2 tablespoons garam masala
1 small red chilli, deseeded and finely chopped
1 large onion, chopped
150ml (5fl oz) vegetable stock or water
250g (8oz) young leaf spinach
250g (8oz) cooked potatoes, diced
125g (4oz) cottage cheese
1 x 20g (³/₄oz) pack coriander, freshly chopped
salt

Heat the oil in a saucepan over a moderate heat, add the garam masala, chilli and onion and cook for 6-8 minutes, stirring occasionally.

Stir in the stock or water and spinach and cook for 2 minutes, until the spinach has wilted.

Add the potatoes and a little salt if liked, and heat through.

Serve topped with the cottage cheese and sprinkled with coriander.

COOK'S TIP
For authenticity, replace the cottage cheese with paneer, a fresh Indian cheese.

aubergine madras

A vegetarian dish that is as good served cold as an accompaniment as it is as a hot main dish.

prep & cook time   serves 4   per serving   per serving

1 tablespoon fennel seeds
2 tablespoons vegetable oil
1 large onion, peeled and chopped
4 cloves garlic, finely chopped
1 teaspoon ground fenugreek
625g (1¼lb) aubergines, cubed
1-3 teaspoons hot chilli powder
1 tablespoon ground coriander
1 teaspoons ground turmeric
2 x 400g (14oz) tins chopped tomatoes
300ml (½ pint) vegetable stock
natural yogurt, to serve

Lightly crush the fennel seeds using a pestle and mortar.

Heat the oil in a large saucepan and gently fry the onion, garlic, fennel seeds and fenugreek for 4-5 minutes until softened but not browned. Stir in the aubergines and stir fry for a further 5 minutes.

Add chilli powder to taste, along with the coriander, turmeric, tomatoes and stock. Bring to the boil, cover and simmer gently for 20 minutes or until tender.

Serve with natural yogurt spooned over, accompanied by poppadoms.

sweet potato and mango jalfrezi

Great for vegetarians and vegans - no compromise on the flavour front here!

25 mins prep & cook time

serves 4

281 cals per serving

7g fat per serving

1 tablespoon vegetable oil
1 medium onion, chopped
1 clove garlic, crushed
2 tablespoons Jalfrezi seasoning
600ml (1 pint) vegetable stock
300ml (1/2 pint) passata
500g (1lb) sweet potatoes, cut into
  1cm (1/2in) dice
500g (1lb) cauliflower, broken into small
  florets
1 red pepper, deseeded and cut into 1cm
  (1/2in) strips
1 mango, peeled and roughly chopped
salt and freshly ground black pepper

Heat the oil in a heavy-based pan. Gently cook the onion and garlic until soft.

Stir in the Jalfrezi seasoning and cook for 3 minutes. Stir in the stock, passata, sweet potatoes, cauliflower and pepper. Bring to the boil, reduce the heat and simmer until the vegetables are tender.

Season to taste. Stir in the mango and serve immediately. Rice and slices of mango make an ideal accompaniment.

chickpea and spinach curry with soft eggs

A one-pot meal that will satisfy the heartiest of appetites.

prep & cook time   serves 4   per serving   per serving

250g (8oz) dried chickpeas
1 teaspoon cumin seeds
2 teaspoons coriander seeds
3 large cloves garlic
450g (15oz) tomatoes
2 rounded teaspoons tamarind paste
150ml (¼ pint) hot water
2 tablespoons groundnut oil
50g (2oz) butter
1 teaspoons ground turmeric
2 teaspoons mustard seeds
¼ teaspoon cayenne pepper
450g (15oz) fresh spinach
4 medium or large eggs
handful fresh coriander leaves, roughly
   chopped
salt

Soak the chickpeas in water overnight. Drain and boil in plenty of water until really soft. This can take anything from 45 minutes to over 2 hours, depending on the age of the chickpeas. Drain well.

Grind the cumin and coriander seeds finely. Peel the garlic and chop roughly. Put the tomatoes in a bowl, cover with boiling water and leave for 2 minutes, then peel and chop roughly. Put the tamarind paste into a measuring jug, add the hot water and stir to mix.

Put the oil and butter in a wide, heavy, heatp casserole over a moderate heat. Then stir in turmeric and the ground cumin and coriande Next add the garlic and chopped tomatoes, t tamarind water, mustard seeds, cayenne pepp and a sprinkling of salt. Add the cooked chickpeas, cover the dish and cook gently on hob, stirring once or twice, for about 15 minu

Meanwhile, wash the spinach and add the wh leaves to the casserole. Cover again and continue cooking for about 5 minutes, until t spinach is soft. Remove the lid and, if the mixture is slightly liquid, let it bubble up for a few minutes, stirring, until it is fairly thick and mushy.

Lower the heat and make 4 depressions in th chickpea and spinach mixture. Break the eggs carefully into these depressions. Cover again cook for 6-8 minutes, until the eggs are just s they should still be runny in the centre. Sprin with roughly chopped coriander leaves and se immediately.

Variation
Use tinned chickpeas if you are short on time

Note
Pregnant women, babies, the elderly and thos who are suffering illness should avoid food wi lightly cooked or raw eggs in them.

tandoori fried fish

A delicately flavoured main course that is perfect for lunch or dinner.

15 mins	serves 4	199 cals	10g fat
prep & cook time	serves 4	per serving	per serving

500g (1lb) firm white fish, cut into 5cm
   (2in) strips
6 tablespoons natural yogurt
1 tablespoon Tandoori masala powder
2 tablespoons vegetable oil
$^1/_2$ red onion, sliced into rings, to garnish
1 tablespoon coriander leaves, to garnish
1 tomato, sliced, to garnish

Lay the fish strips in a large non-metallic dish.

Mix the yogurt and curry powder together. Coat the fish on both sides, cover and chill for 20-30 minutes.

Heat the oil in a heavy-based pan and fry the fish strips for 5-8 minutes, turning once. Garnish with the red onion, coriander and tomato and serve immediately.

COOK'S TIP
**Use any firm white fish fillets for this dish –
cod, haddock and coley are all suitable.**

spicy prawns

Great as a warm salad dish or as a tasty filling for pitta bread.

30 mins prep & cook time

serves 4

157 cals per serving

3g fat per serving

2cm (1in) piece root ginger, grated
1 clove garlic, crushed
1 teaspoon garam masala
1/2 teaspoon chilli powder
1 tablespoon ground coriander
1 tablespoon lime juice
100ml (3 1/2fl oz) thick natural yogurt
50g (2oz) raisins
375g (12oz) raw tiger prawns
1 tablespoon sunflower oil

Mix together all the ingredients except the prawns and oil.

Add the prawns and stir to coat.

Leave to marinate for 30 minutes.

Heat the oil in a frying pan over a moderate heat. Add the prawn mixture and fry for 2-3 minutes until the prawns turn pink.

COOK'S TIP
Raw prawns, which are grey instead of pink, are available at some fishmongers' or fish counters.

mussels masala

Serve with plenty of naan bread to scoop up the spicy creamy sauce.

30 mins		**350** cals	**31**g fat
prep & cook time	serves 4-6	per serving	per serving

500g (1lb) mussels
25g (1oz) unsalted butter
4 cloves garlic, finely chopped
2 shallots, finely chopped
4 tablespoons medium curry paste
300ml (1/2 pint) fresh fish stock
284ml (1/2 pint) double cream
salt and freshly ground black pepper
coriander leaves

Clean the mussels by scraping off any barnacles, detaching any beards and scrubbing the shells. Discard any open mussels that do not close when lightly tapped. Put to one side in a bowl of salted cold water.

Gently melt the butter in a heavy-based pan and fry the garlic and shallots until soft.

Stir in the curry paste and fish stock and bring to the boil. Turn down the heat and simmer gently for 4-5 minutes until the liquid is reduced slightly. Season to taste.

Add the drained mussels to the pan. Cover and cook for 4-6 minutes or until the mussels open. Gently stir in the cream, garnish with coriander leaves and serve immediately.

salmon kedgeree

An extra-special kedgeree - great for feeding a crowd of hungry friends for lunch or brunch.

45 mins
prep & cook time

serves 6

319 cals
per serving

19g fat
per serving

500g (1lb) salmon, filleted and skinned
1 tablespoon white wine vinegar
1 onion, chopped
2.5cm (1in) piece of fresh root ginger, peeled
  and grated
1 clove garlic, crushed
2 tablespoons vegetable oil
1 teaspoon garam masala
2 green chillies, deseeded and finely chopped
4 tomatoes, skinned and chopped
juice of ½ lime
2 tablespoons fresh coriander, chopped
10cm (4in) cinnamon stick
5 green cardamom pods, bruised
2 cloves
150g (5oz) basmati rice
½ teaspoon ground turmeric
pinch chilli powder
450ml (¾ pint) fish stock or water
50g (2oz) seeded raisins
50g (2oz) flaked almonds, toasted lightly
salt and freshly ground black pepper
coriander leaves

Cut the salmon into 4cm (1½in) cubes and toss in the vinegar with a pinch of salt.

Lightly fry half the onion and the ginger and garlic in 1 tablespoon of the oil for 2 minutes. Stir in the garam masala and green chillies and cook for 2 minutes.

Add the tomatoes and salmon and continue cooking until the fish is almost cooked through.

Sprinkle over the lime juice and stir in the coriander. Cover and set aside.

Heat the remaining oil, add the remaining onion, the cinnamon, cardamom and cloves, and fry until golden.

Stir the rice into the pan and fry for 2 minutes, stirring well to coat the rice grains with the oil. Add the turmeric, chilli powder and the fish stock or water and stir well.

Cover the pan and cook for about 25 minutes, until the rice is cooked and all the liquid has been absorbed.

To serve, discard the cinnamon stick and layer the rice and fish in a serving dish. Top with the raisins, almonds and coriander leaves.

prawn kebab pockets

Marinated prawns are a great idea for a relaxed lunch or summer supper.

prep & cook time 1½ hrs serves 4 per serving 608 cals per serving 42g fat

5 green chillies, deseeded and roughly chopped
3 red chillies, deseeded and roughly chopped
2 cloves garlic, peeled
2cm (³/₄in) fresh ginger, peeled and chopped
2 tablespoons lemon juice
2 tablespoons vinegar
1 tablespoon cumin seeds
1 tablespoon garam masala
pinch turmeric
3 tablespoons natural yogurt
500g (1lb) large raw tiger prawns, peeled leaving the tail intact
1 small red pepper, deseeded and cut into chunks
1 small yellow pepper, deseeded and cut into chunks
1 large red onion, peeled and cut into chunks
100g (3½oz) paneer cheese, cubed
100ml (3½fl oz) oil
1 teaspoon mustard seeds
2 large plain naan breads
½ iceberg lettuce, shredded
4 wooden skewers, soaked in water

For the prawn kebabs: Place the chillies, garlic, ginger, lemon juice, vinegar, cumin seeds, garam masala, turmeric and 6 tablespoons of water in a food processor and process until a fine paste is achieved.

Transfer this mixture to a non-metallic dish, t add the yogurt and mix well. Stir in the prawn red and yellow pepper and onion and put to o side to marinate for 1 hour.

Thread the prawns, pepper, onion and paneer alternately onto the skewers.

Heat three-quarters of the oil in a heavy-base frying pan, add the kebabs and cook over a moderate heat for 10 minutes, turning regula to ensure they brown evenly.

Heat the remaining oil in another pan, add th mustard seeds and cook until the seeds begin to pop. (Be careful when carrying out this procedure as the seeds will spit.) Pour the contents over the pan of cooked kebabs.

To serve, warm the naan breads, then cut horizontally and pull apart to form a pocket. Fill with lettuce and top with a kebab. Serve immediately.

Variation
Use halloumi cheese instead of paneer.

chicken korma

A mild and creamy curry that tastes ten times better than the take-away version!

| prep & cook time | serves 4 | per serving | per serving |

1 hr • serves 4 • 639 cals • 24g fat

1.5kg (3¹/₂lb) chicken, cut into 8 pieces
  and skinned
150g (5oz) natural yogurt
2 cloves garlic, crushed
2 teaspoons turmeric
50g (2oz) butter
1 large onion, sliced
5cm (2in) piece fresh root ginger, peeled
  and cut into thin strips
¹/₂ teaspoon chilli powder
1 teaspoon coriander seeds, crushed
5 whole cloves
1 teaspoon salt
5cm (2in) piece cinnamon stick
2 teaspoons cornflour
150ml (¹/₄ pint) single cream
25g (1oz) unsalted cashew nuts, browned
  under the grill

Place the chicken pieces in a non-metallic dish. Mix together the yogurt, garlic and turmeric, and pour over the chicken. Cover and leave to marinate overnight in the refrigerator.

Melt the butter in a large saucepan and cook the onion gently for 5-10 minutes, until softened but not browned.

Add the ginger, chilli powder and coriander seeds and cook for a further 5 minutes.

Add the chicken with its marinade, the cloves, salt and cinnamon stick, cover and simmer for 25-30 minutes until the chicken is almost cooked through.

Blend the cornflour with the cream, stir into the chicken, and continue to cook for another 5 minutes until the sauce has thickened. Sprinkle with the nuts and serve immediately.

balti chicken

'Balti' means 'bucket', referring to the
shape of the cooking pot.

| prep &
cook time | serves 4 | per
serving | per
serving |

3 tablespoons vegetable oil
1 onion, finely chopped
1 teaspoon ground coriander
1 teaspoon ground cumin
1 teaspoon ground ginger
1 teaspoon turmeric
1/2 teaspoon chilli powder
1 garlic clove, crushed
1 courgette, sliced
230g (8oz) can chopped tomatoes
1 teaspoon sugar
4 tablespoons water
500g (1lb) boneless, skinless chicken breasts
   cut into small pieces
1 teaspoon cornflour
150ml (1/4 pint) soured cream
50g (2oz) creamed coconut, chopped
salt and freshly ground black pepper

Heat 1 tablespoon of the oil in a large pan and
fry the onion until soft. Stir in the spices and
garlic and cook for 1 minute.

Add the courgette, tomatoes, sugar and water.
Bring to the boil and simmer for 10 minutes.

While the curry sauce is cooking, heat the
remaining oil in a wok or large frying pan and
stir fry the chicken in batches until golden br
and cooked through. Remove the chicken fro
the pan and add it to the sauce.

Stir the cornflour into the soured cream and
it to the curry sauce, along with the creamed
coconut. Stir until the sauce is boiling and th
creamed coconut has dissolved. Season to ta
and serve at once.

tikka chicken

This tangy chicken dish can be prepared in the morning or the night before and cooked in minutes in the evening.

1¼ hrs
prep & cook time

serves 4

176 cals
per serving

3g fat
per serving

1 teaspoon hot chilli powder
1 teaspoon ground coriander
1 teaspoon ground cumin
2-3 cloves garlic, crushed
2.5cm (1in) piece fresh root ginger, grated
175ml (6fl oz) natural yogurt
1 tablespoon chopped coriander
¼ teaspoon salt
2 tablespoons lemon juice
¼ teaspoon grated lemon zest
4 boneless chicken breasts, skinned
lemon wedges
coriander leaves

Line the grill pan with foil, place the chicken pieces on top and grill for 8-10 minutes on each side, basting frequently with the marinade.

When cooked through, lift the chicken onto a warmed serving plate, garnish with lemon wedges and coriander, and serve immediately.

Put the spices in a large bowl, add the garlic and ginger, then stir in the yogurt, coriander, salt, lemon juice and zest.

Make 3 diagonal slashes in each chicken breast, add to the bowl and spoon over the marinade, ensuring that each piece is well coated. Cover and chill in the refrigerator for 1-6 hours, turning occasionally. The chicken can be left in the fridge overnight for cooking the next day.

Preheat the grill to hot.

marinated lamb chops

A spicy marinade lifts everyday lamb chops out of the ordinary.

1¼ hrs		301 cals	23g fat
prep & cook time	serves 4	per serving	per serving

4 lamb chops
150g (5oz) natural yogurt
1 clove garlic, crushed
1 tablespoon ground coriander
2 teaspoons turmeric
2 teaspoons paprika
juice of 1 lime
1 x 20g (³/₄oz) pack fresh coriander, finely chopped
salt and freshly ground black pepper

Place the lamb chops in a suitable non-metallic dish.

Combine all the marinade ingredients in a bowl and pour evenly over the chops. Leave to marinate in the refrigerator for 1 hour or overnight.

Preheat the grill to hot. Grill the chops for 6-8 minutes on each side, basting occasionally with the marinade.

Serve immediately with a crisp green salad.

lamb chapatis

Herbs and spices combine to make a delicious meal that's great for entertaining.

prep & cook time   serves 6   per serving   per serving

For the marinade:
150ml (¼ pint) Greek-style yogurt
1 onion, finely chopped
25g (1oz) fresh ginger, peeled and finely chopped
2 small green chillies, deseeded and finely chopped
½ x 20g (¾oz) pack coriander, roughly chopped
6 large mint leaves, finely chopped
½ teaspoon turmeric
1 tablespoon ground cumin
1 tablespoon ground coriander
1 teaspoon garam masala

1 tablespoon corn oil
425g (14oz) lamb neck fillets, cut into 2cm (¾in) dice

For the chapatis:
¼ cucumber, cut into 1cm (½in) cubes
¼ red onion, sliced
200g (7oz) tomatoes, deseeded and cubed
½ x 20g (¾oz) pack coriander, roughly chopped
6 tablespoons natural fromage frais
2 tablespoons paprika
6 chapatis

Combine the ingredients for the marinade and stir in the cubes of lamb, ensuring even coverage. Cover, place in the refrigerator and leave to marinate for 30-60 minutes.

Heat the oil in a large frying pan and seal the cubes of lamb on all sides. Reduce to a medium heat and cook slowly for 20 minutes.

To make the accompaniments, mix the cucumber, onion, tomatoes and coriander together and place in a small bowl. Cover and leave to stand so the flavours can develop.

Mix the fromage frais with the paprika and set in another small dish.

Warm the chapatis through in the oven or microwave, following pack instructions. Fill with cubes of cooked lamb, top with the cucumber and tomato mixture, and finish with a spoonful of spicy fromage frais if desired.

lamb, potato and spinach curry

Serve this one-pot meal with lots of naan bread to mop up all the delicious juices.

1 hr	serves 4	382 cals	27g fat
prep & cook time	serves 4	per serving	per serving

4 cardamom pods
1 teaspoon coriander seeds
1 teaspoon cumin seeds
2 teaspoons garam masala
450g (15oz) lean lamb fillet, cut into
    1cm (1/2in) cubes
2 tablespoons vegetable oil
2 medium onions, peeled and sliced
2 cloves garlic, finely chopped
1 green chilli, deseeded and chopped
300ml (1/2 pint) vegetable stock
300ml (1/2 pint) canned coconut milk
450g (15oz) potatoes, peeled and cut into
    chunks
250g (8oz) baby spinach
salt and freshly ground black pepper

In a pestle and mortar, lightly crush the cardamom pods to split the green husks. Prise out the black seeds and discard the husks. Crush the seeds along with the coriander and cumin. Mix with the garam masala and then toss with the lamb in a large bowl to coat it.

Heat the oil in a large saucepan and gently fry the onion, garlic and chilli for 5 minutes until softened but not browned. Add the spiced lamb and cook, stirring, for 3-4 minutes until browned all over. Pour in the stock and coconut milk, bring to the boil, cover and simmer gently for 20 minutes.

Add the potatoes to the lamb, stir well and simmer, uncovered, for a further 15 minutes the potatoes are tender. Then add the spinac and plenty of seasoning. Stir well and cook fo further 2 minutes until the spinach has wilte Serve immediately.

COOK'S TIP
This is a mild creamy curry. To add heat, d with cayenne pepper to serve, or replace th green chilli with a red chilli. To save time, replace the whole spices with ground ones, and use garlic paste and ready-minced chil

coriander meatballs

Quick and simple to prepare, these
meaty morsels are a real treat.

30 mins prep & cook time   serves 4   **295 cals** per serving   **20g fat** per serving

500g (1lb) extra-lean minced lamb
1 onion, chopped
1 clove of garlic, crushed
20g (³/₄oz) fresh coriander, chopped
1 tablespoon olive oil
salt and freshly ground black pepper
finely sliced red onion and green pepper
   (optional), to garnish

Place all the ingredients except the oil and
garnish in a blender or food processor and purée
to a smooth mixture. Shape the mixture into 8
balls and chill for 30 minutes in the refrigerator.

Add the oil to a large frying pan and lightly fry
the meatballs for 20 minutes, turning
occasionally, until cooked and golden.

Remove the meatballs from the pan and drain on
absorbent kitchen paper. Transfer to a serving
plate, garnish with red onion and green pepper
and serve immediately.

vegetables

crunchy beans with fenugreek butter

Add freshness and flavour to your plate with this simple vegetable dish.

20 mins		61 cals	5g fat
prep & cook time	serves 2-4	per serving	per serving

200g (7oz) fine green beans
25g (1oz) butter
juice of 1 lime
1 x 20g (³/₄oz) pack coriander, finely chopped
1 teaspoon fenugreek seeds
salt and freshly ground black pepper

Cook the beans in boiling salted water for 5-10 minutes until tender but still crunchy. Drain and set aside.

Melt the butter in the saucepan and stir in the lime juice, coriander and fenugreek. Tip in the beans and shake the pan to cover them with the butter. Season to taste and serve immediately.

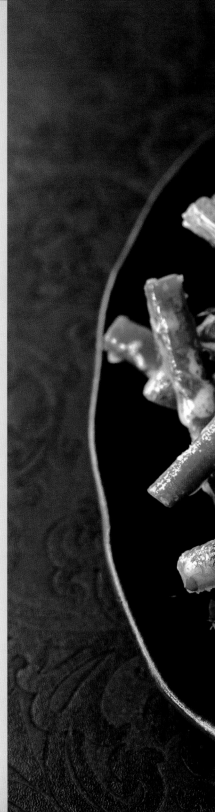

spicy courgettes

Very simple to make, and just as good cold as hot.

30 mins
prep & cook time

serves 4-6

53 cals
per serving

3g fat
per serving

1 tablespoon oil
2 large shallots, chopped
400g (14oz) can chopped tomatoes
2 cloves garlic, crushed
2.5cm (1in) piece fresh root ginger, crushed
   or grated
1/2 teaspoon chilli powder
3-4 courgettes, sliced
salt and freshly ground black pepper to taste
a little chopped parsley to garnish

Heat the oil in a saucepan, add the shallots and cook for 5 minutes, without browning, stirring occasionally.

Add the tomatoes, garlic, ginger and chilli powder. Bring to the boil, then simmer for 20 minutes, uncovered, until thickened.

Stir in the courgettes, season with salt and pepper, and cook for 5 minutes, until just tender. Serve hot or cold, garnished with parsley.

patty pans with coconut and ginger

A touch of ginger gives this lightly spiced vegetable dish a fresh taste.

20 mins — prep & cook time

serves 4

253 cals — per serving

21g fat — per serving

2 tablespoons oil
2 teaspoons ground cumin
2 teaspoons ground coriander
2 cloves garlic, crushed
2cm (³/₄in) piece fresh root ginger, grated
500g (1lb) patty pans, halved
1 bunch salad onions, sliced diagonally
75g (3oz) creamed coconut dissolved in
    150ml (¹/₄ pint) hot water
4 tablespoons freshly chopped coriander
salt and freshly ground black pepper

Heat the oil in a large frying pan or wok, add the cumin, coriander, garlic and ginger, and cook for 1 minute, stirring occasionally.

Add the patty pans and onions and cook for 5-6 minutes, stirring occasionally. Add the creamed coconut, most of the coriander and seasoning to taste.

Simmer gently for a further 5-6 minutes, stirring occasionally, and serve garnished with the remaining chopped coriander.

Variation
Replace the patty pans with other types of squash, such as cubes of pumpkin, butternut squash or marrow.

70

yellow spiced potatoes

A vibrant side dish that will liven up any meal.

30 mins		367 cals	21g fat
prep & cook time	serves 4-6	per serving	per serving

6-8 medium potatoes
125ml (4fl oz) vegetable oil
2 cloves garlic, chopped
1 teaspoon ground turmeric
1 teaspoon salt
1/2 teaspoon chilli powder
1/2 teaspoon ground cumin
1/2 teaspoon mustard seeds

Cook the potatoes whole in boiling water for 25-30 minutes, until just cooked through. Do not overcook. Drain and leave to cool, then cut into bite-sized pieces and put in a large saucepan.

Heat the oil in a small frying-pan and cook the garlic, turmeric, salt, chilli powder, cumin and mustard seeds for 3-4 minutes, until the garlic has browned.

Pour the spice mixture over the potatoes, mix well and heat over a moderate heat for a few minutes, until quite hot. Serve immediately.

spiced fennel potatoes

Chilli and fennel seeds give the humble spud a touch of heat and crunch.

30 mins	serves 4	241 cals	16g fat
prep & cook time	serves 4	per serving	per serving

4 tablespoons corn oil
4 cloves garlic, peeled and crushed
2 teaspoons mild chilli powder
1 tablespoon fennel seeds
500g (1lb) new potatoes, quartered, cooked and refreshed
2 green chillies, deseeded and finely chopped
salt and freshly ground black pepper

Heat the oil in a large frying pan, then fry the garlic for 1 minute. Add the chilli powder, fennel seeds, potatoes and chillies and cook for a further 4-5 minutes.

Season with salt and freshly ground black pepper, and serve immediately.

COOK'S TIP
Replace the fennel seeds with a handful of fresh fenugreek leaves.

sultana and potato bhuna

'Bhuna' is a method of frying spices in oil, which brings out the flavour.

30 mins		**164** cals	**7**g fat
prep & cook time	serves 4-6	per serving	per serving

1 tablespoon vegetable oil
1 red onion, finely chopped
$1/2$ teaspoon ground cumin
$1/2$ teaspoon paprika
2cm ($3/4$in) piece fresh ginger, peeled and
    finely chopped
100g ($31/2$oz) sultanas
300g (11oz) potatoes, peeled, cooked in boiling
    water for 5 minutes, allowed to cool,
    then grated
50g (2oz) unsalted cashew nuts

Heat the oil in a frying pan and cook the onion until softened. Add the cumin, paprika, ginger, sultanas and potato and cook gently for 5-7 minutes.

Stir through the cashew nuts just before serving.

spiced pumpkin and cauliflower

An Indian influence adds an exotic touch to everyday vegetables.

30 mins prep & cook time

serves 4

121 cals per serving

8g fat per serving

2 tablespoons olive oil
500g (1lb) pumpkin, peeled, deseeded and
   coarsely chopped
½ large cauliflower, broken into small florets
1 large onion, coarsely chopped
4 ripe tomatoes, skinned and chopped, or
   230g (8oz) can chopped tomatoes
¼ teaspoon ground turmeric
pinch chilli powder
salt

Heat the olive oil in a large saucepan, add the pumpkin, cauliflower and onion and fry for about 3 minutes.

Add the tomatoes and spices and season with salt.

Cover and simmer for about 20 minutes or until all the vegetables are soft, stirring occasionally.

Variation
Replace the pumpkin with other types of squash, such as butternut or acorn.

cauliflower korma

Serve with other dishes, or double the quantity and serve as a main dish on its own.

30 mins	serves 4	276 cals	23g fat
prep & cook time	serves 4	per serving	per serving

1 tablespoon vegetable oil
1 onion, peeled and finely chopped
1 cauliflower, cut into florets
1 tablespoon korma curry powder
1/2 chicken stock cube made up with 200ml (7fl oz) boiling water
100g (3½oz) creamed coconut
3 tablespoons natural yogurt
20g (¾oz) toasted, flaked almonds
½ x 20g (¾oz) pack coriander, finely chopped

Heat the oil in a large saucepan over a moderate heat and fry the onion and the cauliflower for 4-5 minutes or until browned. Add the korma curry powder and fry for a further 1-2 minutes.

Add the stock, creamed coconut and yogurt, bring to the boil and simmer for 10-12 minutes or until the cauliflower is just tender.

Transfer to a hot serving dish and garnish with the almonds and coriander.

okra stir-fry

An alternative name for okra is ladies' fingers, because of their elongated shape.

20 mins prep & cook time

serves 4

242 cals per serving

18g fat per serving

4 tablespoons sunflower oil
3 tablespoons cumin seeds
2 onions, diced
5cm (2in) piece root ginger, grated
2 red chillies, deseeded and finely chopped
250g (8oz) okra, sliced into 1cm (1/2in) rings
2 tablespoons coriander leaves, finely chopped
1 tablespoon mint leaves, finely chopped
3 tomatoes, chopped into eighths
salt and freshly ground black pepper

Heat the sunflower oil in a large saucepan over a moderate heat. Add the cumin seeds and gently brown. Add the onion and cook for 2-3 minutes until softened.

Stir in the ginger and chillies. Add the okra to the pan, ensuring every piece is lightly coated with oil. Gently mix all the ingredients, and cook for 5-6 minutes, turning occasionally.

Add the coriander, mint, tomatoes and seasoning. Stir well and cook for a further 4-5 minutes.

Serve immediately.

mushrooms in sesame oil

This tasty side dish is on the table in a matter of minutes.

10 mins — prep & cook time
serves 4
120 cals — per serving
12g fat — per serving

3 tablespoons sesame oil
2-4 tablespoons lemon juice, to taste
4 bay leaves, crumbled
1 teaspoon chilli powder
375g (12oz) button mushrooms, sliced
salt

Heat the oil in a saucepan over a low heat and add the lemon juice, bay leaves and chilli powder. Cook for 1 minute.

Add the mushrooms and cook for 3-4 minutes, taking care not to overcook.

Season with salt to taste and serve hot.

green pea curry

Easy-peasy green pea curry is the perfect accompaniment to meat or other vegetable dishes.

15 mins — prep & cook time

serves 6

129 cals — per serving

6g fat — per serving

4 fresh green chillies, deseeded and finely chopped
1cm (1/2in) piece fresh ginger, grated
2 tablespoons vegetable oil
450ml (3/4 pint) water
pinch bicarbonate of soda
asafoetida powder, to taste
750g (1 1/2lb) fresh or frozen peas
chopped fresh coriander
grated fresh coconut, optional
salt

Put the chopped chillies and ginger in a mortar or strong bowl and crush to a paste with a pestle or the end of a rolling pin.

Put the oil, water, bicarbonate of soda and the ginger and chilli paste in a saucepan. Add salt and asafoetida powder to taste, stir well and heat.

When hot, add the peas and cook for 10 minutes until warmed through. The peas should not change colour. Remove from the heat and serve, garnished with coriander and coconut, if using.

COOK'S TIP
Use ready-made ginger and chilli paste to save time.

karahi karela

Karela is an exotic vegetable which looks a little like an elongated gourd.

45 mins — prep & cook time

serves 4

168 cals — per serving

15g fat — per serving

1 teaspoon salt
500g (1lb) karela, peeled and cubed
4 tablespoons oil
1 medium onion
1 clove garlic, chopped
2-3 green chillies
small bunch coriander, chopped
pinch bicarbonate of soda
1 teaspoon ground cumin
25g (1oz) molasses
1 teaspoon turmeric powder
salt

Sprinkle a teaspoon of salt over the karela cubes and leave for 1/2 hour.

Heat the oil in a heavy-based pan or karahi.

Squeeze out the excess water from the karela cubes. Using a food processor, grind the onion, garlic, chillies and coriander into a paste. Add the paste to the hot oil and cook for 3 minutes over a moderate heat, stirring occasionally.

Add the karela, bicarbonate of soda and cumin, stirring occasionally. Cook for a further 10-15 minutes, add the molasses, turmeric powder and salt to taste. Stir in gently to coat the karela. Serve immediately.

lentil-stuffed mushrooms

Serve as an accompaniment to your main dish, or double the quantity to make a delicious lunch or light supper.

1 hr		328 cals	19g fat
prep & cook time	serves 6	per serving	per serving

250g (8oz) green lentils
1 lime, cut into quarters
2 cloves garlic, peeled
1 x 20g (3/4oz) pack fresh coriander
4 tablespoons oil
1 large onion, peeled and finely chopped
1 red pepper, deseeded and chopped
1 yellow pepper, deseeded and chopped
175g (6oz) young leaf spinach
3 tablespoons medium madras curry paste
6 tablespoons water
25g (1oz) unsalted butter
6 open flat mushrooms, stems removed

Place the lentils, lime, garlic and coriander in a saucepan and cover with water. Boil rapidly for 10 minutes, cover and simmer for a further 15-20 minutes. Drain, discarding the lime, garlic and coriander.

Preheat the oven to 190°C/375°F/gas mark 5.

Heat 1 tablespoon of the oil in a large frying pan, gently cook the onion, peppers and spinach for 2-3 minutes, then add the drained lentils, curry paste and water. Cook for a further 1-2 minutes, then put to one side.

In another frying pan heat the butter and 2 tablespoons of the oil and lightly cook the mushrooms on both sides, until coloured. Transfer to a roasting tin, then fill each mushroom cap with the spicy lentil mix. Driz over the remaining tablespoon of oil and coo the preheated oven for 20 minutes.

Drizzle with the pan juices and serve.

chickpeas with raita

Cool down spicy chickpeas with a refreshing yogurt raita.

30 mins		361 cals	15g fat
prep & cook time	serves 4	per serving	per serving

2 tablespoons vegetable oil
1 shallot, finely chopped
2 cloves garlic, finely chopped
2cm (³/₄in) piece fresh root ginger, finely grated
¹/₄ teaspoon ground turmeric
400g (14oz) canned chopped tomatoes
800g (28oz) canned chickpeas, drained and rinsed
2 tablespoons fresh coriander, roughly chopped
2 teaspoons garam masala

For the raita:
150ml (¹/₄ pint) natural yogurt
2 salad onions, finely chopped
10cm (4in) piece of cucumber, cubed
1 teaspoon cumin seeds, toasted
2 tablespoons fresh mint, chopped
pinch cayenne pepper
salt and freshly ground black pepper

Heat the oil in a heavy-based frying pan or wok. Gently fry the shallot, garlic and ginger gently for 2-3 minutes. Stir in the turmeric and cook for a further minute.

Add the tomatoes and chickpeas, bring to th boil, then simmer gently for 10-15 minutes, u slightly thickened. Add the coriander and ga masala and season to taste.

Mix all the remaining ingredients to make th raita.

Serve the chickpeas with the raita on the sic

dhal

Yellow split peas make a creamy dhal with just a hint of a bite.

30 mins	**serves**	**80** cals	**3g** fat
prep & cook time	serves 4-6	per serving	per serving

1 tablespoon olive oil
1 small onion, finely chopped
1 clove garlic, finely chopped
2cm (³⁄₄in) piece root ginger, peeled and
    finely chopped
1 bird's eye chilli, deseeded and finely chopped
250g (8oz) yellow split peas
600ml (1 pint) vegetable stock
20g (³⁄₄oz) fresh coriander, roughly chopped
salt and freshly ground black pepper
mini poppadoms

Place a saucepan over a moderate heat, and add the oil. Fry the onion, garlic, ginger and chilli for 2 minutes. Add the split peas and stock.

Bring to the boil, reduce the heat and cook for 40 minutes until the split peas are tender. Stir occasionally, especially towards the end of the cooking time.

Remove from the heat, add seasoning to taste, stir in the coriander and serve with mini poppadoms.

COOK'S TIP
Grate the ginger on the coarse side of a cheese grater if you prefer.

rice and
bread

pooris

Wholemeal pooris make an ideal scoop for sauces and dhals.

45 mins
prep & cook time

makes 14

197 cals
per serving

18g fat
per serving

150g (5oz) plain wholemeal flour, plus extra
    for rolling
1/2 teaspoon salt
125ml (4fl oz) water
250ml (8fl oz) vegetable oil

Place the flour and salt in a bowl, add the water and mix to a fairly soft dough.

Knead for 4-5 minutes, until soft but no longer sticky.

Turn the dough onto a lightly floured surface, and work and roll it with your hands until you have a long snake of dough, about 2cm (3/4in) in diameter.

Cut off a piece of dough about 2cm (3/4in) long, and wrap the remaining dough in cling film.

Work the cut-off piece of dough between your palms until it forms a small, neat ball.

Coat with flour, then roll out until you have a small, flat patty about 8cm (3in) in diameter. Continue cutting and shaping the dough in this way, always keeping the pieces of dough covered with cling film when not being worked.

Heat the oil in a wok or large frying pan unti enough to brown a cube of bread in 30 secon and deep-fry the pooris, one or two at a time making sure you don't overcrowd the pan.

Cook each batch for 2-3 minutes, until lightly browned, turning them once and splashing th with hot oil to make them puff up.

Drain on kitchen paper before serving warm.

potato breads

An easy and delicious alternative to conventional breads.

prep & cook time | makes 15 | per serving | per serving

250g (8oz) potatoes, unpeeled
175g (6oz) plain flour, plus extra for rolling
pinch salt
concentrated butter, ghee or vegetable oil
   for frying

Cook the potatoes in boiling water for about 15 minutes, until just tender.

Drain, leave to cool slightly, then peel and grate into a bowl.

Add the flour and salt to the potato and mix to form a soft dough, adding a little water if necessary.

Divide the dough into 15 small pieces and dust with flour.

Roll out each piece thinly on a lightly floured surface, making rounds of about 15cm (6in).

Heat some concentrated butter, ghee or oil in a large frying pan and shallow-fry the potato bread pieces, in batches, turning once, for 1–2 minutes, until tinged with brown.

Drain on kitchen paper before serving.

pilau rice with cashews

A great spicy accompaniment for any meat or fish.

30 mins		78 cals	7g fat
prep & cook time	serves 6-8	per serving	per serving

2 tablespoons oil
4 shallots, finely chopped
1 teaspoon ground cumin
1 teaspoon ground coriander
1/2 teaspoon chilli powder
6 cardamom pods
2.5cm (1in) piece cinnamon stick
1 blade mace
2 cloves garlic, crushed
250g (8oz) basmati rice
600ml (1 pint) chicken or vegetable stock
50g (2oz) cashew nuts, roasted
salt to taste
coriander leaves to garnish

Heat the oil in a large saucepan, add the shallots and cook for 10 minutes, stirring occasionally, without browning.

Stir in the spices and cook for 5 minutes, ensuring that they do not burn. Add the garlic and rice and cook for 5 minutes, stirring constantly. Pour in the stock, season with salt, cover and simmer for 15 minutes, stirring occasionally, until the rice is tender and the stock has been absorbed.

Transfer to a warmed serving plate, sprinkle with the cashew nuts and garnish with the coriander.

vegetable pilau

A mildly spiced rice dish
which complements meat
or vegetable dishes without
overpowering them.

30 mins		108 cals	4g fat
prep & cook time	serves 6	per serving	per serving

1 medium onion, peeled and finely chopped
1 clove of garlic, crushed
1 tablespoon corn oil
2 teaspoons ground cardamom
1 teaspoon turmeric
6-12 cloves, to taste
1 teaspoon ground cinnamon
100g (3¹/₂oz) cauliflower florets
100g (3¹/₂oz) frozen peas
50g (2oz) sultanas
175g (6oz) basmati rice, rinsed

In a large saucepan, soften the onion and garlic
in the oil, then add the spices and fry for 1
minute.

Break up the cauliflower into tiny pieces, and add
with the peas and sultanas to the pan. Stir for
half a minute, then add the rice and 300ml
(¹/₂ pint) water.

Bring to the boil, stirring occasionally. Cover with
a tight-fitting lid and simmer for 15 minutes. Stir
occasionally, adding a little more warm water
during cooking if necessary.

Transfer to a large bowl and serve immediately.

green pea pilau

This colourful rice can be served as a side dish or as a main course in its own right.

 40 mins
prep & cook time

 serves 6

 484 cals
per serving

 25g fat
per serving

125ml (4fl oz) vegetable oil
2 small onions
1 cinnamon stick, broken up
1cm (1/2in) piece fresh ginger, chopped
1/2 teaspoon chilli powder
pinch ground turmeric
1/2 teaspoon cumin seeds
1 teaspoon salt
about 750ml (1 1/4 pint) water
375g (12oz) long-grain rice
250g (8oz) fresh or frozen peas
25g (1oz) butter

Heat the oil in a large saucepan over a moderate heat and chop one of the onions finely. Fry the chopped onion, cinnamon, ginger, chilli powder, turmeric, cumin seeds and salt for 10 minutes.

Add the water and bring to the boil. Add the rice, cover, lower the heat and simmer for 15 minutes. Next, add the peas and cook for a further 10 minutes, until all the liquid has been absorbed and the rice is tender and fluffy. Add a little more boiling water if necessary.

Meanwhile, melt the butter in a frying pan over a moderate heat and slice the remaining onion. Fry for about 10 minutes, until brown and crisp, stirring frequently. Just before serving, spoon the hot onion and butter over the top of the pilau.

egg and almond stir-fry

Serve this tasty rice dish as part of a larger meal, or on its own for a light lunch.

1 hr	serves 4	695 cals	43g fat
prep & cook time	serves 4	per serving	per serving

250g (8oz) long-grain brown rice
4 tablespoons sunflower oil
1 small or medium-size green cabbage, shredded
1 clove of garlic, finely chopped
125g (4oz) almonds, shelled
1 teaspoon hot Madras curry powder
1 teaspoon ground turmeric
6 hard-boiled eggs, chopped

Cook the rice in lightly salted water for 30-35 minutes or until just tender. Drain, run cold water through and drain again.

Heat the oil in a wok or very large frying pan over a high heat. Add the cabbage and garlic and stir fry for approximately 3 minutes or until the cabbage begins to soften.

Stir in the almonds, rice, curry powder and turmeric and cook for a further 2 minutes. Mix in the eggs and serve immediately.

red lentils and rice

Lentils are a great source of low-fat protein and make an economical but tasty side dish.

prep & cook time	serves 6	per serving	per serving
1¾ hrs		308 cals	8g fat

500g (1lb) basmati rice
250g (8oz) red lentils
3 tablespoons oil
2 tablespoons tomato purée
½ teaspoon turmeric
2 cloves garlic, crushed
1 tablespoon ground cumin
salt and freshly ground black pepper

Wash the rice and soak it in salted water for at least 1 hour. Pick over and wash the lentils and drain both the rice and lentils.

Heat 2 tablespoons of oil in a heavy-based or non-stick pan, stir in the tomato purée and add 1 litre (1¾ pints) water. Add salt, pepper and turmeric, stir well and when it comes to the boil put in the lentils. Cook with the lid on, over the lowest heat, for 10 minutes then add the rice and cook for a further 10 minutes, until all the water has been absorbed, adding more boiling water if necessary.

Fry the garlic quickly in the rest of the oil until it is barely coloured. Stir in the cumin and when the aroma of the garlic and spices rises, pour the garlic mixture over the rice and lentils and mix in with a fork.

warm citrus basmati salad

An easy way to liven up a simple rice salad.

30 mins		**120 cals**	**1g fat**
prep & cook time	serves 4	per serving	per serving

300g (10oz) basmati rice
zest and juice of 1 lime
zest and juice of 1 lemon
20g (³/₄oz) coriander, finely chopped
100ml (3¹/₂fl oz) natural yogurt
salt and freshly ground black pepper
lime wedges to garnish

Cook the rice for 15-20 minutes or according to pack instructions until cooked through.

Stir in the remaining ingredients except the lime wedges, adding salt and pepper to taste and reserving a sprig of coriander. Serve immediately, garnished with the lime and remaining coriander.

sweets

almond sweetmeats

These dainty morsels are perfect with coffee at the end of a meal.

30 mins		380 cals	27g fat
prep & cook time	serves 4-6	per serving	per serving

275g (9oz) blanched almonds
125g (4oz) soft dark brown sugar
1 egg white
caster sugar for coating

Pound and grind the almonds in a pestle and mortar until they become an oily mass. Alternatively, grind the almonds in a food processor, or chop, then grind in batches in a blender until oily.

Turn the ground nuts into a bowl, add the brown sugar and knead thoroughly, until the mixture is very smooth and soft. Add the egg white as you do this to help the mixture stick together.

Divide the almond mixture into 4-6 portions and roll each into a ball. Lightly coat the balls with caster sugar, and roll each one out thinly, into a round.

Place on a piece of muslin or a clean tea towel and leave to dry for 6-8 hours.

Wrap the pieces of sweetmeat individually in greaseproof paper and store for up to 2 weeks in an airtight container.

hot fruit salad

Spice up fruit salad with this luscious syrup and exotic fruits.

30 mins		**290** cals	**0.6g** fat
prep & cook time	serves 6	per serving	per serving

For the fruit:
1 large ripe mango, peeled and cut away from
   the stone
250g (8oz) fresh lychees, peeled and pitted,
   or 1 x 565g (18oz) can lychees, drained
1 large pineapple, peeled and cut into chunks
1 just-ripe pawpaw, peeled, deseeded and cut
   into slices
4 passion fruits, halved
4 apple bananas, peeled and halved on the
   diagonal

For the syrup:
175g (6oz) granulated sugar
1 star anise
1 bay leaf
1 cinnamon stick
2.5cm (1in) piece fresh ginger, peeled and
   finely chopped
grated zest and juice of 1 orange
grated zest and juice of 1 lime

Begin by making the syrup. To do this, place all
the syrup ingredients, except the orange and
lime juice, in a saucepan, along with 600ml
(1 pint) of water.

Place over a low heat until the sugar has
dissolved, then increase the heat and simmer for
5 minutes.

Cool slightly and add the orange and lime jui

Place all the prepared fruit into 4 large soup
bowls and pour the syrup over.

Serve immediately, topped with cream if des

banana lassi

A refreshing drink to serve before, during or after your favourite meal.

30 mins	serves 4	91 cals	1g fat
prep & cook time	serves 4	per serving	per serving

1 large banana, peeled and cut into chunks
250g (8oz) low-fat natural yogurt
125ml (4fl oz) milk
1 tablespoon sugar, to taste

Place all the ingredients in a food processor and process until smooth. Pour into individual glasses and serve immediately.

Alternatively, store for up to 1 day in a refrigerator.

peach salad

Rose-water adds a flowery note to this exotic fruit salad.

20 mins — prep & cook time

serves 4-6

63 cals — per serving

27g fat — per serving

8 fresh peaches, peeled, stoned and sliced, or canned peaches in juice
2 tablespoons rose-water
4 teaspoons sugar
a few saffron strands, soaked for a few minutes
juice 1 lemon
4 tablespoons water
mint leaves, to decorate (optional)

Combine all the ingredients in a large bowl and chill in the refrigerator for an hour.

Serve decorated with a few mint leaves, if desired.

index